For Yolanda,

An old friend
& great supporter
of my creativity.

Love,

Barbara Ehrenwein

Also by Barbara Eknoian

Chances Are: a Jersey Girl Comes of Age

Jerkumstances

Why I Miss New Jersey

by

Barbara Eknoian

Everhart Press

Long Beach, California

Book design by John Stacy
Cover illustration: From a 1950s' Advertising Poster for Palisades
Park, New Jersey

Everhart Press
Long Beach, California
www.everhartpress.com

For my husband, Raymond Eknoian,
my children, and grandkids,
who make every day a blessing,
and sometimes, a delightful surprise.

—

Acknowledgments

The author wishes to thank the editors of the following
publications, both print and electronic, in which some
of these poems first appeared: *Chiron Review, Pearl,
Westview: A Journal of Western Oklahoma,
Your Daily Poem, Palisades Park Art & Poetry Folio,
El Dorado Poetry Review, Silver Birch Press,* and
River Poets Journal. Some of the poems have appeared in the
chapbook, *Jerkumstances* published by Pearl Editions.

Also, with special thanks to Donna Hilbert,
my mentor, encourager, and poetry
workshop leader, who always
generously shared her knowledge with us.

And for all the members of Hilbert's
Tuesday night poetry workshop
for their loyal support.

Also to Marilyn Johnson of Pearl Publications
for her expert help and advice.

CONTENTS

Foreword

Before Springsteen, before "The Real Housewives of New Jersey," there was the Barbara Eknoian's New Jersey of "plaid shirts and chino pants," "pleated skirts and jumpers," sock hops, diners, and soda jerks. There were "the projects," numbers runners, flirty waitresses, and rumors of the mob. Growing up, getting married, moving west, birth, death—it is all here.

The story began in *Jerkumstances (PEARL EDITIONS, 2002)* continues in *Why I Miss New Jersey,* a full and immensely satisfying book: a memoir in poems. C.S. Lewis says, "A pleasure is not full grown until it is remembered." And neither is pain. Barbara Eknoian remembers it all, pleasure and pain, with accuracy as sharp with the mysteries of adult misbehavior, sadness, as with the joy of first dances, first loves. She transforms memory into art. From "15th Birthday":

> Mom is still working,
> so I hint to Dad,
> who is preoccupied
> reading the horse
> racing results.
> Distracted, he reaches
> into his pocket,
> hands me a twenty
> to shop for my present,
> and to buy my own cake.

If Eknoian remembers with accuracy, she also remembers with empathy. From "His Night Life":

> In our family album, there are hardly
> any shots of my father,
> but I recall my favorite picture of him:
> he's standing with his friend, Puggie,
> who'd just got back from the service.
> They're leaning against the bar,
> holding shot glasses high in the air.
> He looks happy in the darkness of the cabaret,
> his face illuminated.

Teaneck, Green Croft, Hopatcong, Bergenline, Bayonne, there is poetry in the names of the New Jersey places Eknoian has loved and left. Though never having been there, I miss them too. Again, I think of C. S. Lewis: "We read to know that we are not alone." Take *Why I Miss New Jersey* with you wherever you travel and you will not be alone, you will have a new best friend between the covers of a book.

Donna Hilbert
Long Beach, California, 2013

Why I Miss New Jersey

Ghost House

Palisades Park, New Jersey

I heard our former New Jersey home
was demolished to make room
for a two-family.
The driveway and garage are gone.
I wonder if the new owners
kept those old license plates
that lined the garage walls?
The Cavallo's are the only hold-outs
on the block, and choose not to sell
their colonial, now dwarfed
by three-story buildings.

Many nights, in dreams, my spirit crosses
the country and hovers over our old address
longing to see where my family was happy.
I see my kids asleep in their beds,
the next-door neighbors around
our dining room table,
my husband dealing out the cards
to play Spades. It's Vivian and me
against the guys.

We often laugh when our husbands

accuse us of cheating.

Jerry prefers a dry martini,

and we sometimes have wine.

Like wearing soft, flannel pj's,

I'm comfy in our married life.

We are naive about our future.

I can't visualize the big move yet,

even when Madam Florence tells me,

"I see you residing in a ranch house."

Lost and Found

There wasn't enough room
in the U-Haul.
We abandoned our first
cream-colored kitchen table,
which still resides back east
at my cousin's house,
and boxes of Bradley's
Dress Store clothing,
made of materials I don't see,
or can't afford anymore:
matte jerseys, organza
and fine sheared woolens.
My wedding gown
of French satin,
with wine spots on the hem,
a pearl gray coat
with a silver fox collar,
and my father's brown fedora.

But those were just things.
I left behind precious people,
my mom, recently widowed,
my 14-year-old kid brother,

my maiden aunts, used to me
dropping by to visit.
My friends next door,
a daily fun part of our lives,
and I left a lot of me.
When my brother mails me
a package,
I'm thrilled to find an 8 x 10
framed sepia photo of my dad
wearing his brown fedora.
And then I notice his smile;
it was so much like mine.

An Elegy for Mom

Mom, on my way to lunch today,
I grabbed a Glamour magazine,
flipped the page open to a model
posed with the back of her skirt
caught up and tucked
under her white underwear.
For the article, she pretended
she was unaware, to see if people
would be kind enough to let her know.
Catcalls emerged from passing cars
on the busy Manhattan street,
there were snide remarks from
younger girls, but a percentage
of older women and a smaller group
of men did inform her.

I laughed out loud when I saw the pictures
because they reminded me of the time
you crossed the avenue in West New York
with your dress tucked up into your undies.
I was horrified when you told me,
but you laughed it off saying,
"Hell, I don't know them. They don't know me.

At least, I was wearing underwear."
I recall another time late at night
when you waited at a bus stop
after working at the beauty salon,
carrying bags of capes to wash at home.
A sailor asked you to show him
how to use the pay phone.
You got into the booth to help him
and he crammed behind you
suddenly closing the door,
but you managed to escape.

When you told us the story
we were all doubled up with laughter.
You admitted you were more embarrassed
than scared because he was so much younger.
It never occurred to you he had a motive.
I can still see you shrug your shoulders
and hear you say,
"I'm just a victim of jerkumstances."

For Dad

Rising while we were still asleep
you put your heavy boots on
and left to work the oil fields
fitting iron pipe,
while your hands froze
under the cold, New Jersey sky.
When we awoke we ate oatmeal,
put on our warm clothes,
and hurried to school.
Afterward, we played Hide'n Seek,
Hopscotch, or rode around
the neighborhood
on our shiny, Schwinn bikes.
Still you were not home from work.

On humid, summer weekends,
you dropped us off at the Arcola Pool
out in the suburbs, where we splashed,
swam and cooled off
under the spray of the huge fountain
while you returned to sweat,
over the never-ending repair
to our old house

often pouring yourself some Jim Beam
in your iced coffee to keep you going.

As you hammered and sawed
to improve our lives,
did you ever wonder if it was worth
the sacrifice?
Did our little gifts of Old Spice and ties
really show you
how much we cared?

50s' Backyard Show

Mid-July and we decide
to have a show in my backyard.
The stage, a raised wooden platform,
where we store our bikes
is hidden under a heavy canvas.
For one of the numbers,
I wear a tight purple skirt,
a fur foxtail around my shoulders
and vamp across the stage singing,
"I walked down the street
like a good girl should . . ."
My friend Joanne, is almost six feet tall
so she plays the boy part.
We sing, "He followed me
down the street
like I knew he would . . ."
My eyes catch Mom and Aunt Terry
cracking up at the upstairs window,
but I figure they're enjoying the show.
For our finale, five of us don raincoats,
rubber boots, and carry umbrellas
while our brothers, Robert and Jo Jo
stand high above us

to sprinkle us with watering cans.

Energized by applause, we shout,

 "We're singing in the rain"

over and over

as we don't know all the words.

The Ice Man's Wife

I walk by the TV and see
a Home Box Office documentary
titled, "The Ice Man Tapes."
A killer is being interviewed
at Trenton State Prison, New Jersey.
It holds no interest for me.
I'm on my way to the laundry room.
I stop when I hear a familiar name.

The Ice Man's wife sits
alongside a tranquil lake.
She tells the reporter
she knew nothing about
the drug dealing, pornography,
and his Mafioso contract killing.
Old home movies show scenes
from their past:
opening presents under their tree,
his wife pushing their kids
on the swings, posing
with their parish priest.

The camera pans in on a driveway.

I recognize Vincent's Garage

where the crimes took place.

The Ice Man admits he murdered the man,

then stashed the body into a barrel drum.

The place is across the street

from my grandfather's house.

His wife is my friend from third grade.

Their priest was my parish priest.

Clueless

Just west of New York City
where everyone sounds
like a character from "Guys & Dolls,"
bookies stand on the corner
by Al's Candy Store and Vic's Garage.
Seventy-year-old Mrs. Bennetti
passes a few dollars to my mom
to play her favorite number combo
so her sons won't know she gambles.

On a warm, spring day, three
of my eighth grade classmates and I
wear the same pink
Jonathan Logan dresses to school.
Later, there's gossip that they
were hijacked from a truck.
Someone sold them to the peddler
on Hudson Boulevard.
Mom warns, "Better not wear
that dress to school anymore."

My father is out of work.
I am clueless that he and his pal, Nicky,

are taking horse racing bets
in our downstairs spare room.
When I arrive home from school,
I spot my brother's kiddy whistle
lying on the floor, pick it up
and impulsively blow it hard.
My father throws open the door
cursing in his booming voice,
You stupid bastard. What the hell
are you doing?

When I see his rage,
I am certain he's going
to have a hemorrhage right
in the middle of our hallway.

An Elegy for Marlon

You motorcycled into my heart when I was only fourteen, and you
were *The Wild One.* No one looked as good as you did in your black
leather jacket. In *On the Waterfront* I was mesmerized and proud you
led the dockworkers to victory. I can still hear you yelling, "Stella,"
in *Streetcar Named Desire.*

When I saw you with Jean Simmons in *Guys and Dolls*, I was ready
to become a soldier in the Salvation Army. After you married, had
children, and bought an island in Tahiti, I kind of forgot about you
for a while. Then in *The Godfather,* I was saddened to see how you
aged and gained weight.

The Biography Channel reveals you admired your mother, who acted
in local theater. Both of your parents were alcoholic, and you had to
rescue your mom from bars, and once you protected her from a
beating by holding a .45 to your father's head. At military school,
your teacher encouraged you to try theater, and you excelled on
stage. Your boyhood friend was Wally Cox. You remained best
friends, although you appeared an unlikely couple. He seemed frail,
and you looked strong, but your link was that you both came from
unhappy homes.

While living in Beverly Hills, your daughter became pregnant by one of your island friends. You sent your son to speak to him, but tragedy happened instead, and her boyfriend was killed. You spent millions to defend your son, but he wound up in prison. You said, "In life, sometimes you have to duke it out." A friend tried to cheer you up, and you answered: "How am I supposed to feel? My daughter has killed herself, my son is in prison and my only grandchild's father is dead."

When you died, your family sprinkled your ashes in Death Valley and Tahiti, along with Wally Cox's ashes, which you had kept for thirty years. You received an Oscar for *On the Waterfront*, but refused an Oscar for *The Godfather*, sending an American Indian to protest the poor treatment of Indians in the movie industry. You remain a guiding light for other male actors who study your portrayals of Zapata, Napoleon, Don Corleone, and Colonel Kurtz.

As Marc Antony you spoke over Julius Caesar's body in your strong Shakespearean voice: "And the elements so mixed in him that nature might stand up to say to all the world this was a man," can be repeated by all who knew you best. "This was a man."

Anthony

One afternoon when I was six, Nancy,
my 12-year-old babysitter, took me down the block
to stand in line with other neighborhood kids
in front of an old wood-framed building.
We entered through creaking double doors
and made our way up the rickety stairs
in the dark, musty hallway,
marching in pairs behind the older kids
to the front room of a third floor apartment.

Anthony wore his dark blue Communion suit.
His eyes looked sad, like Sandy,
my cocker spaniel's eyes.
An older lady lay very still, dressed in light blue satin,
face powdered white with rosy-rouged cheeks,
auburn hair styled in finger waves.
Nancy whispered, *Don't say anything; she's dead.*
I didn't know what to do, I just followed Nancy's lead
She knelt and made the Sign of the Cross; I knelt too.
Then, I followed Nancy out into the sunlight.

Soon after, Anthony moved across town.
Through my school years, I sometimes saw him.

He was a box boy at the A & P

and always looked very serious carrying out groceries.

I was just a familiar face; he really didn't know me.

But the image of him standing sad-eyed

dressed in his dark blue suit,

next to his mother dressed in ice blue satin

stuck in my mind like cotton candy.

One day, I saw him sitting on a stoop

with a pretty curly-haired girl.

It was the first time I noticed his dimples.

The Neighborhood

I live on busy Hudson Boulevard
where umpteen buses pass by
on their way to New York City
or Journal Square.
There isn't a flower in sight.
Mom calls it a concrete jungle.

So I play around the corner
in the projects where green
grass grows and leafy bushes
trim brick apartments
that look like rows and rows
of army barracks.

In summer, the project janitors
open up a shower in the center
of the kiddy park to cool us.
We romp in and out of spray.
On a grassy slope we place towels,
then search for four-leaf clover,
but only find three leaf clovers
and scraggly yellow dandelions.

When the blizzard hits in '49
cars can't pass through streets.
We pile on my Flexible Flyer sled
to coast down snowy Jungle Hill.
We play for hours until we're
so cold and our leggings
are soaked with snow or pee.

I walk home dragging my sled
past houses where snow drifts
are as high as first floor windows.
My father surprises me and carves
out a hollow in the snow pile
in front of my house.
Buses whiz by,
but I am safe in my igloo.

The Alvin Theater
Gutenberg, NJ

When I was a kid, before reality set in,
I loved to go to the movies and pretend
I was Cyd Charisse and could dance
with Gene Kelly, or sail along
On Moonlight Bay as Doris Day.
Rock Hudson was Adonis,
and John Wayne, a cowboy
or World War II hero.
Esther Williams, lovely in flowered
bathing caps, swam like a goddess.
I never saw guys dressed as girls
until Tony Curtis and Jack Lemmon
starred in *Some Like it Hot*.
Randolph Scott was the strong, silent
cowboy before I learned
he lived with Cary Grant.
At the movies, 50s' bedroom scenes
had twin beds, then the movie faded out,
when it was time to go to sleep.
Shirley Temple and Margaret O'Brien
were child stars, and June Allyson played Jo,
the favorite sister in *Little Women*.

Hollywood was where Lana Turner

got discovered sitting at a drug store counter,

and Grace Kelly turned into a Monaco princess.

For less than a dollar, I could attend matinees

and sit through the movie twice.

When the theater darkened,

I'd watch

as the projector's light became stardust.

At the House Next Door

the little boy turns the knob
and lets himself in.
He climbs the staircase
surprising his neighbor.

She invites him to walk
to the market with her.
He tells her, "We throw
pennies under the porch
cuz' the elves live there."

Each day at three,
he's her honored guest
as they feast on Rocky Road
and chocolate chips.
He's quick to show her
the margarine bowl he sprayed
with gold paint and macaroni.

When things get dull
at his house,
he saunters over there
where he's treated as a prince.

Suddenly he's transplanted
across the country.
On his first day of kindergarten
he tearfully asks,
"When are we going home?"

At the house next door
the knob won't turn.

Blue Mountain

We hike down the curved dirt path
behind the red brick projects,
with their rows and rows
of clotheslines,
holding our noses as we pass
the small dairy,
with the awful manure smell.
We're on our way to play
on the cliffs half-way between
the buildings above us
and the main highway below,
crowded with trailers and cars.
At the base of the cliff,
stands a tall rock, three stories high,
called Blue Mountain
because it's tinged blue
from the smoky emissions
of the old dye factory.
We hike to the bottom of the cliff,
then scale the granite mass
stepping carefully into grooves,
and little crannies to make it
to the top of the mountain

where there's a flat surface

dubbed the King and Queen's Seat.

Nearby our brothers,

King Arthur's knights,

duel with wooden swords.

We survey our kingdom,

until the factory whistle blows.

Cookie

1952 - We meet at Mc Gowan's Camp. She dreams up an act
for me to do for the talent show. It's a toss up between
a radio jingle about Campbell's Pork N' Beans, or the
Irish lullaby, Tura-Lura-Lural.

1956 - I bump into her again at Palisades Amusement Park.
She's working at the soft ice cream stand. She always
gives me a free cone.

1957 - We wind up at the same high school. She's the only girl
in our class who drives a car. We all pile in and drive
to Callahan's for hamburgers.

1958 - She invites two of her guy friends to ride along with us.
We drive through Hudson County Park. They ask her
to stop for a minute at the bowling alley to tell their pals
they're going out with us. While they're inside, I get
cold feet. I yell, "Step on it, Cookie. I don't want to go
with them." The car screeches out of the parking spot
as we make our getaway down Bergenline Avenue.

1959 - We leave the prom and head for The Barn in Greenwich
      Village. I drink too much Singapore Sling. In the picture,
      Cookie's tiara is on straight and mine is lop-sided.

1960 - Cookie, Betty, and I go to a drive-in to see Psycho.
      During the shower scene, we are scared out of our minds.
      We scream and rush to roll up the car windows and lock
      the doors.

1961 - I catch her leaving the Lora Lei Dance Club with Red,
      the policeman, who had asked me out the week before.

1962 - I can't leave my wedding reception for my honeymoon
      because someone says, "Cookie is missing." I find her
      sitting in a ladies' room stall asleep.

1969 - We attend our ten year reunion. My husband and I help her
      home and put her to bed.

2006 - I try to locate her on Classmates.com. Instead, I notice
      a familiar name. I contact the person and ask, "Are you the
      same Richard, who owned a motorcycle shop on Grand Avenue,
      and is married to Cookie? He responds, "Yes, I am.
      But sadly, Cookie passed away last winter."

   (With thanks to Deborah Harding)

Dance

Union City, NJ

The summer after 8th grade
we plan to attend our first dance.
I'm filled with questions:
what to wear
and how to style my hair.
I go over to Debbie's house
to borrow a matching cotton
skirt and blouse.
I trust her judgment;
she's been to a modeling class.

As we approach St. Michael's,
I'm ready to change my mind.
I have to be pushed inside.
The kids stand in clusters
in the dimly-lit gym.
We nervously chat
in our small group of four.
Then a blue-eyed guy,
who could be a junior or senior,
asks me to dance.

We circle the floor slowly
to Nat King Cole's "A Blossom Fell."

When the dance is over,
I stand dazed
in the center of my friends.
I've just stepped into my teen years.
My hair upswept in a French twist,
dressed in pink organza.

The Green Croft

In my sixteenth summer, I worked
at The Green Croft, a family inn,
green-shuttered, four stories high
right on Lake Hopatcong.
After supper, we'd congregate
on the front porch,
rocking back and forth in our chairs,
like old grannies while the rich kids
whizzed by in their speed boats.
Across the lake, the Bon Air Lodge
was lit up like an electric power house,
with a band playing every weekend.
We envied the tourists and wished
we were older to venture
across the River Styx Bridge
to attend their big Labor Day bash.
On the porch, the ancient juke box
housed only one modern song.
I played Elvis's
"I want you, I need you, I love you,"
over and over
pining for a boy back home.

One night, Charlie, a guest who looked

like a forty-year-old bookworm,

sat at the upright piano and played,

"A Whole Lot of Shaking Going On"

as good as Jerry Lee Lewis.

Guests pushed the ping pong table aside,

started to rock n' roll.

Peter the waiter tried to pull me up

to Lindy, but I was too shy and said no.

He grabbed Kathy, the waitress,

flipping her around like the "Swing Kids."

I sat there and felt the floorboards

vibrating beneath me

as Charlie banged the piano

and pumped on the foot pedal below.

Dancing at The Y.W.C.A.
Bayonne, NJ

Recently married, we venture
with a small group of friends
to learn *Ballroom*.
As we enter the hallway
the lively music lures me.
My heart beats a bit faster
anticipating the dance.
Then our lessons begin.
Men line up across the floor,
mimic the male teacher's steps.
Ladies stand on the other side,
follow the female instructor.
We get together with partners
mouthing to each other one, two,
one, two, three to Cha Cha,
and one, two, three
one, two, three to Waltz.

Winners of the Harvest Moon Ball,
our teachers perform for us.
Lino, graceful and lean, instructs us
in his sexy Italian accent.

47

I'm in awe, imagine dancing with him:

We Quick Step across the floor,

then glide like ice dancers

to a Viennese Waltz.

Even in my mind, there's trouble

following his lead,

to the Tango's staccato beat.

I want to wrap my leg around his knee.

It's hard to keep the Samba's *t*empo.

swaying our hips, taking swift steps.

For the final dance,

Spanish music inspires us

to march out for the Paso Doble,

hear the roar of the crowd

awaiting the bull.

I swing my red satin cape

in swirling arcs;

he thrusts his sword.

Diner

On Friday nights, we'd have
the Blue Plate Special prepared
by Greek short order cooks.
Miniature silver jukeboxes
hung above Formica tables
in each window booth.
I'd ask Dad for some quarters
to play the Platters or Presley.
The clatter of dishes
and the crowd in the diner
seemed to awaken my father
as he reached out to shake hands
and wave to old friends.
He'd often pick up the tab
thinking it was expected of him.
I'd wonder about all the dollars
he'd thrown away on strangers
on playing the numbers and horses
as I watched cigarette smoke
curl over the patrons' heads.

That night, I noticed
the brassy red-headed waitress

holding a carafe of coffee,

wink at my father, then walk away

with a sure-of-herself wiggle.

Jake the Boxer flirted

with the blonde, married waitress.

Sultry Vera was out

for a night on the town.

I imagined musky odors floating

above cheap motel beds.

I thought of my mother

at home with the baby,

a yellow layette blanket

wrapped snugly around him.

Double-Hearted Gold Pin

In my bureau drawer,
in a green velvet ring box,
I keep a tiny,
double-hearted gold pin
with mother-of-pearl inlaid
on top of the gold,
engraved with my father's name,
Charles, on the left heart.
On the right heart of the pin,
the pearl topping
which would've read
Viola, is lost.
When I hold the hearts
in my hand,
I see a fun-loving couple
on a three-day honeymoon
enjoying the stroll
on the boardwalk at Atlantic City.
Their future looking as bright
as the glassy, white sand.
Yet, I know it was grittier
than smooth.
Looking closer at the pin,

I wonder when
my mother's heart was lost.
It disappeared somewhere
as though she couldn't bear
more pain, with the arrow
going straight through the heart.

15th *Birthday*

Bergenline Ave., West New York, NJ

It's my birthday,
and I know for sure
my parents will order
a whipped cream cake
from Rispoli's Bakery,
until I'm aware
there's no fanfare
for my special day.
Mom is still working,
so I hint to Dad,
who is preoccupied
reading the horse
racing results.
Distracted, he reaches
into his pocket,
hands me a twenty
to shop for my present,
and to buy my own cake.
Walking alone on the avenue
I enter Guy's Records,
browse through
the single 45's,

choose "Teenage Prayer,"

a mournful song,

as I'm love sick

for a high school senior.

Then I stop

at the Daylight Bakery,

select chocolate cake.

On my way home,

I'm wondering

what happened.

Before, I could

always count

on my parents

being there

as sure as the moon

appears

every night in the sky.

First School Days

On my first day of kindergarten
I feel grown-up and wonder why
a kid a head shorter than me
is pulling me by the hand into class.
I listen to the boys talking
about getting soap in their eyes
when they take their baths.
I see girls fighting about
who should push the baby buggy.
At recess we play
"The Farmer in the Dell" and I think
I don't want to be "the cheese."

In first grade, I'm late for school,
can't open the big heavy door.
I walk home crying and a fireman
from the firehouse walks me
back to school and opens the door.
My teacher, Miss Smith, still yells at me.

In second grade, Mrs. Grant calls me
to the front of the class to ask why
I missed school the day before.

I look around at my classmates
and burst into tears.
I was told when the whistle blew
there was no school due to snow.
The teacher was just kidding with me.

On my first day of high school
I feel grown-up and sophisticated
although I can't find my friends at lunch.
I've gotten lost all morning looking
for classrooms so I hike to my aunt's house
fearing I might have to sit alone in the gym.

Then I become a re-entry student at college.
I walk around campus alone searching
for classrooms and I feel as though
I've just arrived at kindergarten.

Another Side of Life

If you look past the poverty
of the town,
the run-down houses,
the oil-stained streets,
view families through
their lighted windows
see them laugh
while watching TV,
you might see
another side of life,
another kind of beauty.
Watch the young father
reach out to steady
his baby's first steps.
See the mother,
shoulders bent, leaning
over the kitchen table
to help her children
with their homework.
She hopes
they'll surpass her
in their education,
be able to raise

their children
in the suburbs
choose to break bread
with their brothers
because they'll always
be there for each other
If you look past the poverty
of the town, and picture
future prospects,
then you might see
another kind of beauty.

Good-bye Summer Buddy

For the past three summers we work
together as waiter and maid
at Lake Hopatcong's Green Croft Inn
He used to tease and call me "Johnny Mop,"
Now it's "Emmy Lou," the lanky teenager
in the cartoon who wears bangs and a pony tail.
It's our last summer and we shadow each other;
guests say they can see a change in us.
Every night we sit on the porch playing Elvis'
"Don't be cruel" and "I Want You, I Need You,
I Love you," the only modern songs
in the ancient jukebox.
We hate the ham salad sandwiches our boss makes
for lunch every day so he throws them away.
We head for the ice cream shop in the village,
and often break curfew to walk miles for pizza.
Every night we talk for hours about our crushes.
He tells me why he thinks some girls are too fast.
Yet, he hopes he has sex before the Pope opens
that letter in 1960 since it might be a prophecy
that the world is coming to an end.

It's our last Labor Day at the hotel
but he has to leave early for football practice.
It's hard to say good-bye to my summer buddy.
I stand in the hotel hallway sobbing,
my shoulders shaking, my tears flowing non-stop.
I know we'll lose touch; life is moving us on.

In my spirit, I'm resisting like a little kid
who doesn't want to leave her mommy
to attend kindergarten.
I'm about to be captured, tied to a desk
at Mutual of New York, typing insurance claims.

Happy Days

West New York, New Jersey

It was the year of pleated skirts and jumpers,
orlon sweaters, and puffy sleeved blouses,
boys in plaid shirts and chino pants.
We looked as if we stepped out
of a Sears catalog.

Mornings, we ran for the cross-town bus
to get to Memorial High School on time.
On our way home, we'd hike two miles
to stop at Lynn's Ice Cream Parlor
for ice cream or milkshakes.

One lunch hour at school, news spread:
James Dean killed in a car accident.
Some of the girls were shocked
and gathered in groups crying
for the dreamy rebel who died so young.

It was the last of the "Happy Days" era.
At parties we drank soda,
long before Coke became a drug.

We couldn't foresee the future;
younger brothers and sisters
who would get hooked on heroin
and some who would die from AIDS.

His Night Life

We should have saved the 8 x 10 glossy
of Dad and his friend Joe
with Sammy Davis Jr., Al Martino,
and Sophie Tucker at a night club
in Cuba, just before the revolution.
The last time I saw the picture,
it was stapled to the wall
behind his tool bench in the basement.
It was one of the few times,
he'd posed without his Fedora,
revealing his bald head.
With his big smile and warm handshake,
I imagine him sending a round of drinks
to their table, then asking
if they'd pose for the photograph.

Another time, at the Copa, he engaged
Bob Hope in conversation, because
he noticed him trying to place
where he had known him.

My dad jokingly bet Hope
his diamond watch
that he wouldn't remember.
He had caddied for him in 1939,
thirty years before.

In our family album, there are hardly
any shots of my father,
but I recall my favorite picture of him:
he's standing with his friend, Puggie,
who'd just got back from the service.
They're leaning against the bar,
holding shot glasses high in the air.
He looks happy in the darkness of the cabaret,
his face illuminated.

Holding On

I don't throw away
old address books.
There's a history
in their pages.
People I once knew
and lost touch with
since I moved away.
Family members
who have died,
friends, who are
no longer Mr. & Mrs.
and I wonder
what happened
to them.
When I turn the pages,
a familiar name
might cause me to recall
school days, a wedding,
a christening,
or maybe even a funeral.
I've always been
too sentimental
holding on to things.

Some may

have forgotten me,

but I don't want

to forget them.

How can you toss out

a memory?

I preserve

the address books

as though a family album.

They're not going

anywhere.

They'll be safe with me.

Homesick

I cross the miles holding
on to memories:
my children's first steps,
their first days at school,
their romps in piles
of orange and gold leaves.

The neighborhood movie house,
where Rocky played
for six months,
was something I could rely on
when I looked up at the marquee.

The drugstore where my kids
brought their piggy banks,
the clerk counting out pennies
for them to buy me perfume.

Chatting with neighbors
over the backyard fence,
as we hung clothes on our lines.

Margaret always washed
on Mondays, shopped on Thursdays;
Vivian walked to the market at noon.

I arrive in the new land
of smog-filled haze
and star-like cacti--
I am on another planet.

I long to see the familiar landscape
of windswept leaves
resting against
the sagging redwood fence.

Innocence

My best friend, Mary and I,
sat through the movie twice.
We cried so hard that a stranger
passed us some Kleenex.
As we left the Embassy Theater,
the wet wind lashed
around our legs
and blew our hair
in all directions.
Holding a huge umbrella
over our heads
we walked arm and arm
down the avenue
wearing our red rubber boots

We window shopped at Shirlane's,
Corduroy Village, and Little Marcy's,
pretending we'd come back
to buy the fuzzy angora sweaters
and the plaid pleated skirts.

Some boys rode by, whistled,
then hollered, "Lezzies!"
We quickly unlinked our arms
and shouted back, "Jerks!"

I don't recall the name of the movie
we saw that day.
But I'll always remember wading
through puddles
laughing and talking
huddled under our umbrella.

Billy Boy

I remember Billy Boy
racing down the street,
always in the lead,
his blonde curls flying.
He liked to watch Captain Video
and the Video Rangers with us
since his parents didn't own a TV.

After the fire at Miller's place,
they sent him away to reform.
He fell for Tanya,
the town's teenage floozy,
and they had a litter of kids.

There were rumors
Tanya slept around
while Billy Boy worked nights
on an assembly line
at the Christmas ball factory.

He started drinking and drugging.
They caught him running naked
down the boulevard shouting,
"I'm the Messiah!"

After shock treatments,
he wore a "Happy Face"
and shook hands with everyone
asking, "How the hell are you?"

When Tanya's male friends
became too much for him,
he moved to a cellar apartment
to live alone.

One day they carried him out
on a gurney.
No one knew how many days
he'd been dead.

Let-Down

At the pizza parlor after the dance
the boy I like confides to his friend.
He wants to walk Diane home,
but knows that I have a crush on him.

I don't know where I get the courage,
but I go over to his table, sit down
and tell him it's fine with me.

On the way home with my friends,
I hold back tears, then I say
goodnight and run up the stairs.
I look out my bedroom window.
There's no stars out tonight.

I need my mom, but she's working
the night shift at Howard Johnson's.
Dad overhears me crying and asks,
What's wrong?

Between sniffing, I tell him
I like a boy, but he likes my friend.
Dad looks relieved and hugs me.

My head rests on his shoulder.
He says, *Honey, you're young;*
there will be other boys.

I feel as though I just confessed
to Father Fanelli.
I want Danny.
I need my mom.

Lincoln School #5
North Bergen, NJ

Every Wednesday
I dreaded entering
the drab auditorium
to attend music class.
Ms. Henderson's voice,
ruined years before,
croaked like a frog.
She stomped her foot
and shook her fist
when we didn't follow
her commands.

Then the neighborhood
held a talent show
at Lincoln School.
We strolled the stage
dressed like peasants
pretending it was
a village in Italy.

An older man crooned
Mama in Italian,
and some wiped the tears
from their eyes.
We laughed when Rosie,
dressed in a sailor suit, sang
Josephina please don't
leana on the bell.

Bright lights, gaily colored
costumes, and tambourines
transformed the stage
forever in my mind.

The chorus sang,
Finicule, Finicula,
and we danced
the Tarantella.

Louie the Shoe

At the edge of Meadow View Projects, climbing
down a slight slope, we enter the north side
of Flower Hill Cemetery.
We're ten-and eleven-year olds playing
on the green leaf-shaded paths,
bordered by rose bushes and azaleas,
happy to escape the hot asphalt streets.

Marble tombstones surround us;
some have angels on their headstones.
We see a rusted metal crib at the top of a slope.
The inscription reads Nancy Benson,
born February 2nd, 1895, died May 4th, 1895.
The gardeners leave water cans around
so we water the infant's neglected grave,
unaware our meager sprinkling
would not do much, but our hearts are tender,
and tears come easy.

There are warnings not to walk around
because Louie the Shoe roams
about the cemetery with his two large hounds.
He carries his BB gun over his shoulder,

looking for kids playing at Flower Hill.
One summer day it's almost twilight
when we hears dogs barking.
Someone hollers, "It's Louie the Shoe."
Five of my friends scamper up the slope
to return home leaving me standing alone
at the bottom of the hill, my body
in a frozen pose like I'm playing Statue.
Carl climbs back down
and drags me up the incline.

When my grandson wants to hear a scary story,
I tell him about Louie the Shoe
prowling the pathways of Flower Hill.

Monday's Child

He arrived five days before my first birthday
so I learned to share early. Mama said I was
Friday's child loving and giving.
As toddlers we slept in a double bed.
He drew an imaginary line and warned,
"Don't cross it."
At camp, I spent my allowance carefully
so on the bus ride home I'd have a treat.
The lady at the snack window said,
"Sorry your brother used up your money."
I was a spelling bee whiz,
he was dyslexic.
Every lunch hour, Mama played a record
and we'd hear, "A-Apple B-Banana,"
but phonics escaped him.
Most teachers called me into his class
to take home notes to my mother.
He dropped out of school,
related to the Hippie movement,
experimented with drugs, tried LSD,
and stayed with marijuana.
He was Monday's child, fair of face.
When he walked into a crowded room,

someone said, "He's beautiful.
With that beard he looks like Jesus."
He surpassed me reading Philosophy,
hated to hear about the imbalance
of power in the world.
Football players and Johnny Carson
making millions made him go into a tirade.
He could've out-talked the radio hosts.
Now he lives at a shelter, and called me to say
he contracted HIV from a lady he'd been with.
I'm horrified thinking she probably tricked him,
but he says,
 "No, we were just two lonely people
out drinking,
who needed a warm body to feel close."

Moving

I've recently lived in Toronto,
Laguna Niguel,
a Florida condo,
at a family inn,
a large home on a hillside,
and on the street where
my former house
has been knocked down
to make room for a duplex.
My favorite neighbors
usually live right next door.
The homesick feeling
has disappeared like smoke
above a bonfire,
but the ashes reside
in my subconscious.
I can't go back to what was;
I regret impulsive moves
across the country.
Last night, I wandered down
a street lined with small shops.
People gathered to wait
for the parade to begin.

I looked up
at the bannered arch
with huge printed letters
that welcomed me
to *Somewhere*

Mrs. Cox

Taught us how to subtract
in story form showing how John
had to borrow from Mary, and
Mary had to borrow from Tom.
In between each subject, she'd stop
and tell us a story, sometimes
from the newspapers
and sometimes fiction.
It was in her class that I first heard
about Lizzie Borden
chopping up her parents.

Mrs. Cox's sausage fingers
displayed beautiful penmanship
on the blackboard.
She often looked messy,
with wispy gray hairs
slipping out from her bun.
She always showed concern
for all of her students.
When my mom wrote a note
that I had a hard time breathing
because of allergies,

Mrs. Cox cut out an ad
of a hospital bed on sale
thinking it would help me to sleep.

After high school,
I ran into her at the bus stop.
She remembered my name
and started to tell me a story
about one of her students
who had just gotten married.
Before she could finish,
the bus pulled up,
and I was left standing there
wanting to hear the ending
just like I did in third grade.

Muller's Drug Store

In the store at 61st and Hudson Boulevard,
Charlie, the druggist, would go behind
half-shuttered doors to fill prescriptions,
a yellow light hanging over his steel gray head.

One summer day, I bought a box of raisins,
then poured them on to a paper plate
to share with my best friend.
There were little worms crawling all over them.
I hurried back to the drugstore,
stood on tip-toe at the counter, held out the box
complaining, "There are worms in here."
"Good," he said. "We'll have meat tonight."

My mother insisted he was a brilliant man,
that he had a sad life,
and when she'd go to the drug store
she'd get lost for an hour talking to him.
My father painstakingly drew her a map
to show the way home,
which was only half-way up the block.

When it was that time of the month,

I dreaded walking into Muller's

past the teenage boys who hung out there.

I'd whisper, "Modess."

Charlie would continue conversing with the boys,

while he carefully wrapped my package

with newspaper, He never carried paper bags.

I wished I could creep out as quietly

as the cats that sat on the tops

of the many cardboard boxes

lined up in the aisles of the store.

My Mother Tells Her Story

I am three living at Auntie Anna's house
in Long Island because Mama, a single parent,
has to work in a factory during the week.
One Sunday, a visitor brings me a porcelain doll
with brown braids and shiny amber eyes.
I sit in the parlor as the grownups talk.
I am sleepy and the nice man
carries me up the stairs.
I rest my head on his shoulder
holding on to my dolly with my other hand.
He tucks me in and kisses me on my cheek.
Lying in my bed, I hear the hum of voices below,
so I creep quietly out of bed and see my Auntie
saying good night to the nice man.

Years later, I am a mother with three teenagers,
when my Aunt Anna comes to visit me
all the way from Virginia.
I ask, "Was that man,
who gave me the doll, my father?"
Smiling Aunt Anna only says,
"Yes, that was Bob.
He was such a gentleman."

Like a quilt maker, I piece it together:
Mom had woven a story that my father
was Robert Smith, a sailor, who died at sea
when I was a baby.
I close my eyes and try to remember it all.
He picks me up, carries me up the stairs.
I notice his palm is injured,
crushed somehow, but I don't know why.
I see him putting on his winter coat.
He notices me peeking down at him
and smiles from the foot of the stairs.

Night Sounds

The wail of the distant train comforts me
when horns stop honking in the night
I'm just a little girl tossing in my bed.

I hear the train clacking down the track
and the whistle echoing from far away
The wail of the distant train comforts me.

Climbing up from Hackensack meadowlands,
the sound creeps into my bedroom window
I'm just a little girl tossing in my bed.

Moonlight slips through the worn-out shade
Where is Mommy? I hear her crying.
The wail of the distant train comforts me.

I'm afraid and listen to the night sounds
I hear the phonograph playing downstairs.
I'm just a little girl tossing in my bed.

I'm dreaming I can fly far-far away
I wake up when the grown-ups shout
The wail of the distant train comforts me
I'm just a little girl tossing in my bed.

On a Snowy January Day

I shop at Macy's
and find myself browsing
through cruise wear selections.
I'm enchanted
by a black bathing suit
with a satin border
sewed under the bust line.

I enter the dressing room
and try on the suit knowing
I'm not going to Miami.
I should be shopping
for a warm winter coat,
but it's fun to try it on
when you're the right size.

Now so many years later,
I avoid the dressing room,
usually guess at my size,

rather than undress
in the cubby hole
with lights from hell
shining down creating
moon craters on my thighs.

Our Old Address

North Bergen, NJ

My father buys a run-down
turn-of-the-century house
with a storefront window
on the first floor, and a black
iron stove in the kitchen.
All the windows,
are rickety and drafty.
The sixteen stairs creak.
There's a bull's head hanging
over a spare room door.
He remodels a small bedroom
into a pink-tiled bathroom.
and converts two rooms
into one living room.
Three high windows replace
the storefront so that people
passing by can't peek in.

In the fifties and sixties, he spends
his married life fixing the house,
He sweats through summers,
pours whiskey into his iced coffee,

while he saws, hammers and paints.
He could have moved to the suburbs,
but the house has a hold on him.
It's rebuilt with his muscles and tears.
After he dies, Mom gives it up,
needs the money to live on.
There's no longer a family home.
I imagine his ghost can't rest.
He wants to fix the old bathroom.
His footsteps climb up the stairs
from the musty basement.
He's looking for Seagram's Seven
stashed in the kitchen cabinet
to pour into his coffee mug.

Playing God

For Dad, I'd choose a saintly woman,
eager to please, a good cook,
who would be a role model
for her children.
Even though he didn't believe,
it might've brought order
and peace to his life.

For Mom, I'd find her old beau,
Warren, who walked miles
from Secaucus in a snow storm
just to see her.
Every morning, he'd leave for work
and remember to kiss her good-bye,
They would never go to sleep angry.

My brothers and I would have
high self-esteem and solid careers,
like a caring social worker,
a Diane Sawyer reporter,
or, an actor like Robin Williams
who could make his audience
laugh or cry.

We would break the curse
of family addictions
and never dabble with drugs.
Yes, if I could go back
and change the scheme of things,
I'd do it in a flash –
with the blink of my eye.

On Saturday Mornings

I hurried around the corner to play
with my friends in the projects.
Kids chalked the concrete
to play a game of hopscotch.
Boys lined up for stickball.
Mothers stood in the square,
alongside bushels of wet clothes
to hang up on the lines
Parents passed by with grocery carts
on their way to the A & P a mile away.
The candy store thrived with neighbors
having a hamburger and cup of coffee.
In good weather, parents sat
on benches gossiping with friends.
We were never lonely.
We all knew each family by name.
We had room to jump rope,
ride our bikes, and to go sledding
down Jungle Hill during winter.
Neighbors looked out for each other.
There were no guns or drugs.

Then the pushers came in the night

selling heroin to younger brothers

and sisters. One by one families

were hit with addiction,

and the shock of loved ones

dying of AIDS.

Filled with low income families,

the project was never Shangri-La,

but it was a happy place to grow up.

How did the devil manage to infiltrate?

Who let him in?

Runaway

Mom folds the wash, listens
and takes my brother's side
of the argument.
I feel they're ganging
up on me.
As I walk away,
they both laugh.
I'm convinced God
must have given me
to the wrong family.
I gather some clothes
and stuff them into my red,
white and blue skating case,
take a few dollars
from my secret stash
under my bunk bed,
stomp down the stairs
and slam the door behind me.
They're not going to have me
to pick on anymore.

I cross Hudson Boulevard and sit
at Jessie's Sandwich shop,

just a narrow store with a counter,
stools, and a pie display case.
I choose pumpkin pie
since it tastes like Grandma's.

With each bite, I wonder where
I should go next.
It's closing time, almost 9 p.m.
Then I realize it's Monday night,
so I head for home
because I can't miss
"I Love Lucy."

Safe Journey

We drive north on the highway
heading for Reno.
My husband urges me
to put my seat back to rest.
I close my eyes and feel
my body sway gently side to side
with the tires spinning
against grooved pavement.
The rocking motion transports me
back to my father's 1950
powder blue Packard.

We are going south to Miami.
My baby brother is asleep
on the back seat
scrunched up against Robbie,
and I am lying in the back
on the floor, an army blanket
draped over us.
I look out the window and see
the blackest sky filled

with blinking stars
as white as my brother's
bleached diapers.

The radio is playing up front.
I hear a strong voice singing,
"He's got the whole world
in his hands,
the whole wide world
in his hands."
I rock gently back and forth,
my body curled over
the carpeted drive shaft,
knowing someone
is holding us right
in the palm of his hand.

Salon Reflections

Under the hairdryer,
without my bifocals on,
I gaze across the beauty salon.
I see beautiful shades
of sparkling sherry,
shimmering blond,
and amber brown
framing blurred faces.

Everyone is lovely.
Everyone is equal.
There is no discrimination.
I have an inkling
of what heaven must be like.
I linger under the hairdryer
twenty minutes longer
tentatively
holding back reality.

Saturday Confession
Our Lady of Liberia

On our way to confession, we search our souls
for sins we committed during the past month.
Comparing notes, we classify them
as venial sins: talking back to our parents,
fighting with our brothers, and telling lies.
Mary-Margaret prompted, "Don't forget
you went to a Protestant Church last Sunday.
That's practically a mortal sin."

I kneel in the confessional, whisper
through the screen, my grocery list of sins.
Just to make sure
I'm making a good confession, I declare,
"I attended a Protestant Church last week."

The priest's gown rustles. He leans closer
to the window and asks,
"Didn't you know it was a sin?"

"But, I said my own prayers."

"The Catholic Church is the one true church,"
he admonishes.

"But nobody knew I was Catholic."

From the confessional, I emerge in tears,
to face a long line of penitents.
Their knowing looks confirm,
the priest, undoubtedly, has heard
a significant confession.

Scenes from Another Life

I'm wheeling my baby brother
down the boulevard in his
baby carriage. He smiles angelically.
I walk along and imagine
what a fine boy he will be.

A phone call in the present time:
"The police just took your brother
for a 72-hour hold to USC lockup."

Dad's proud of their change-of-life baby.
He hitches a ride home
with the stewardess, then brings her
in to show off his infant son.

Today, my brother sobs in front of my door.
He says we don't understand him.
I'm controlling his money.

At eleven, he's on the stage
singing and dancing the soft shoe.
For his first and only commercial,
he pretends to be a young boy
locked up because of drugs.

I say, "Mom and Dad wouldn't want me
to give you money to kill yourself."
He asks, "So you're communicating
with the dead these days?"

I'm at wit's end not knowing how
to cope with his sadness.
I seldom drink, don't smoke,
never dabbled with drugs.
I search for Apricot brandy
in the back of the closet,
and pour myself a big drink.

Serendipity

I waited my turn at the Serendipity Salon
in Teaneck, New Jersey,
for Michel, the French Canadian
to style my hair.

He charmed me, chatting feverishly
in his lovely French accent,
as he performed magic with his scissors.
I emerged feeling just like Jackie Kennedy.

He went south to seek his fortune
and there were always Michel stories
buzzing around the crowded salon.

He drove a Mercedes,
lived in an oceanfront condo
in Boca Raton ,
and he was supposedly kept
by a wealthy Palm Beach man.

Until, one day, a patron announced
Michel had died from AIDS.
The stylists held their dryers

and combs in mid-air,

a woman interrupted

her sip of coffee,

someone turned down the volume

on the radio,

and there was a moment of silence

at the Serendipity Salon in Teaneck.

Shalimar

I spray cologne on my wrist,
smell the spicy, sweet fragrance.
At once, I'm stepping
out of a taxi
dressed in a tight sheath,
black fur jacket,
about to enter the Lora Lei
on New York's eastside.

I pass guys lined up at the bar
wearing Brooks Brothers
suits and ties.
I smell Canoe as I walk by.
The oomp-pah-pah band
strains to play a cha-cha.
Smoke hovers over the tables
and my friends wave for me
to join them where they
are surrounded by several
of New York's finest.

It's Friday night
and I dance till 2:00 a.m.

My partner hums
"For all we know
we may never meet again."
I smile because we're strangers
just enjoying the dance.
I place the perfume
back on the shelf,
breathe deeply.

Snowfall in the City

From my second floor kitchen,
I would sit on a high stool,
looking out our wide window
watching people pass by
on their way
to the post office next door,
the butcher shop,
or Muller's Drug Store
on the corner.
There was the smell of diesel
from the buses,
sounds of honking horns,
the slam of the post office
truck's door,
and a constant parade of cars.

When it snowed late in the night,
traffic slowed to just a few cars.
The island that separated
north and south bound traffic
had tall, silver lampposts
shining their light on the slant
of the lusty falling flakes.

Then, I could see this was how
it should be, sacred and holy;
the busy boulevard turning
into another world, white as clouds,
hiding grime below its blanket of snow.

Summertime

I remember when summertime seemed like forever.
We neighborhood kids stayed outdoors late to play.
The warm, sunny days lingered past twilight.

We hung out at the park in the Meadowview Projects
Sitting by the monkey bars, seesaws and swings.
I remember when summertime seemed like forever.

Our parents smoked and gossiped on wooden benches
While we played Kick-the-Can and Hide and Seek.
The warm sunny days lingered past twilight.

Every night the white ice cream truck jingled its bell.
We begged for money, and then chased it down the street.
I remember when summertime seemed like forever.

Sometimes we played Truth, Dare or Consequences
And the boys figured out how to steal a kiss.
The warm, summer days lingered past twilight.

We thought we would always be friends
Not knowing how far we would wander away.
I remember when summertime seemed like forever
The warm, sunny days lingered past twilight.

Sunbeams of 1953

My best friend from grammar school
mails me a photocopy
of a dance recital program titled,
"Sunbeams of l953,"
and at once I'm racing up the stairs
to Miss Barry's School of Dance
with Ruthie, Francie and Mary.
It's Christmas time and we sing-a-long
to "I saw Mommy Kissing Santa Claus,"
as we hurry to tie our tap shoes,
hustle into class, and line up
in front of the mirrored wall.
We are in awe of Miss Barry
in her black leotard, her hair
pulled back smoothly in a chignon.
We learn one dance step a week.
She calls out "Scuff heel,
toe heel step. Scuff heel,
toe heel step," and we make
tapping sounds with our shoes.
Nino plays the piano. We tap
to "Crazy Rhythm" and I imagine
I'm leggy Cyd Charisse.

Since I am the tallest,

I'm the boy lead in the Mambo.

My friends ask if we can be a trio

of boy dancers, because they like

the costume of green satin capris.

Recital fever sparks the air.

We perform three numbers,

ballet, tap and jazz

at the Park Theatre

on 32nd Street in Union City.

We are the "Sunbeams of 1953."

That Last Summer

Lake Hopatcong, NJ

We pushed off from the dock
in a canoe at dawn,
the sky blushing pink,
the lake water still as a pond,
no speedboats splashing by,
all the boat docks deserted
as vacationers were sleeping.

With every stroke of the paddle,
I noticed his strong muscles
and I knew I would miss
our tug of war trying to push
one another into the lake
in the evenings after supper.

The solitude was broken
when we laughed
as a muskrat swam by.
Then we glided
under the River Styx Bridge
to Byron's Cove,
where some huge estates

showed no signs of life.

We guessed the owners

had found more exotic places.

But I was so content to be there

on the lake

with my best summer buddy

for our last summer together

that I photographed

the landscape in my mind.

If it had not been so beautiful,

I would've forgotten it by now.

The Beatitudes

We are rounded up at the projects
by a Salvation Army team
who takes us in an old station wagon
to Vacation Bible School.
At 9 years old, it's the first time
I hear Scripture. When they recite,
Blessed are the poor in spirit
and *Blessed are those who mourn*
for they will be comforted,
I don't know what the words mean,
but it sounds beautiful to me.
When there's an altar call,
I don't know what it is,
but I feel an inner nudge to go forward.
I'm the only one in my group
to kneel at the altar.

Now, when I add a volume
of "The Best American Poetry"
to my collection,
which I've bought annually,
I'm troubled to see the first poem
refers to "The Beatitudes"

using vulgar slang
to describe a woman's anatomy.
Just like the day so many years
before when I responded
to the altar call,
I feel an inner nudge.
I sense it's right for me to rip out
the first page of my new poetry book
and tear it into little pieces.

The Democratic Club
North Bergen, NJ

At Frankie's Italian Restaurant,
the neighborhood is in attendance
for a Democratic political bash.
My Dad wants to be committee man
to help get people out to vote.
At the bar, I notice he's speaking
to a woman, his old flame,
my mother's former friend.
They haven't seen each other
since their affair thirty years ago.
They're making small talk,
until I get up and sit on the seat
right between them.
They both look warily at me.

I'm feeling like a virgin since
this is my first time to sit
on a bar stool in a tavern.
I pretend I've done this before,
but I'm not sure whether I pay
for the drink, or if the bartender
will put it on my dinner tab.

I don't make eye contact with Dad.

because I fear he wants

to wring my neck.

Then his former dalliance flirts

with another man.

My mission accomplished;

I return to my table

with my ginger ale.

The Man in the Moon

I am dazzled by his full,
white face so round and bright
in the dark sky.
We haven't communed in years.
When I was a child, I would note
that sometimes he looked happy,
sometimes sad.
He holds my gaze and seems
to be telling me a story:
I was here before you were born.
I'll be here long after you're gone
shining down on your children
and grandchildren
as I did for your grandparents
all the way back to Adam and Eve.
So don't fret, take a deep breath,
enjoy my moonlight.
Although most of the stars
are hiding tonight,
I promise there are more
than you can imagine
stippled throughout the universe.
Tonight I'm your man in the moon

whispering only to you.

When it's your time, follow my light

and swirl among the stars

on your way

to your heavenly journey.

The 70s'

Palisades Park, NJ

We bought our first house and met
Jerry and Vivian, older than us,
but younger in spirit.
They liked a good time, took us
along for the ride where we
enjoyed the town pool,
a poor man's country club.

Every other Saturday night we attended
pool dances under the open pavilion.
The girls dressed in long skirts,
dangling earrings, and poufed their hair.
The men wore sport jackets and ties.
One night the lively crowd
shouted out the lyrics to
"Joy to the world, all the boys and girls,"
everyone swayed to the music.

When I call back east to see how
my old friends are doing,
I'm not ready to hear Jerry is ill.
Vivian says he doesn't want chemo.

I hang up the phone and can't erase

from my mind the lively couple,

who took us to night clubs,

played Spades at our house,

and partied with us every New Year's Eve.

No matter how much time goes by,

I remember Jerry, suave

like a young Frank Sinatra.

He's feeling mellow from his second martini.

The lights flit across Viv and Jerry's shoulders

as they circle the dance floor.

They are the 70s'.

The Summer of Possibilities

I entered Lake Hopatcong's
only ice cream parlor.
He was standing behind the soda fountain
and I noticed his white blond hair.
Just so I could see him every day,
I ordered sundaes, apple turnovers
and banana splits.
By summer's end, I had gained ten lbs.
One day he canoed past our hotel dock
looking for me,
but I had gone home for the weekend.
Many nights that winter I fantasized
how I would be more outgoing
and by summer
I'd land a date with him.
I arrived at the lake on a sunny
June morning and he whizzed by
in his pink convertible with three friends.
Later, I entered the ice cream parlor
expecting to see him, but found out
he had just left for the Navy.

That summer, every time I heard
"Tears on my Pillow"
on the radio
I cried for him.

The Visit

Paramus, NJ

Some of the residents sit outside
in their wheelchairs
in the hot, humid air with no breeze.
He prefers watching old movies
on a TV that his social worker
gave him because she knows
he needs a diversion.
He has three roommates
who don't communicate.
They're burned out
and have lost their minds.
An old man across the hall
shouts over and over,
 "Help me. Be a sport, help me."
The doctors say my brother
doesn't belong in this place,
although he is ill with HIV
and has to live on the county.
I'm miles away in California
It's been six years
since I've seen him.
His eyes are dark;

his body is thin.
He doesn't mention
that his T cells are changing.
I show him family photos
and he laughs out loud
at one black and white 8 x 10
of my mom and her two friends,
waitresses, working the night shift
in the fifties at Howard Johnson's.
He says, "They could've been
a sitcom like Alice on TV."
It hurts to leave him behind
But, he smiles, holds me tight, and says,
 "Hey, thanks for stopping by."

The Waitress

West New York, NJ

It's 2 a.m. at The Star Diner.
The waitress pours coffee
for the cab driver
at the counter on his break.
She banters with her customers
about politics and local gossip.
She's a new widow who never
had to work before,
with a few years left to retirement.
Her family has scattered:
A daughter moved across country,
her son joined the Marines.
The waitress raises a teenage son
alone and worries
that she's lost control.
She used to shop at elegant stores;
now she hurries home to wash
her uniform for next night's shift.
She used to buy filet mignon
from Sam the butcher;
now she serves franks and beans.
Customers have no idea

that their pleasant waitress,

who trades quips with them nightly,

is struggling to get by.

She is good at hiding her fear.

When she gets home,

she'll sit in the recliner,

rest her legs, and count out

the sparse tips from her pockets.

The Window

I wanted our house to be sunny
so when we remodeled
we put in a huge window.
This allowed our next-door-neighbors
a view of our room, as they
were situated a little higher on the hill.
While Vivian washed dishes at her sink,
my eight-year-old, Jill, danced
to West Side Story, unaware she was
entertaining the family next door.

I used to see Vivian shake the dust mop
out her window, and hear Aznavour
playing on her stereo in the background.
When she carried out a basket of clothes
to her backyard, I'd join her to talk
while we both hung out our laundry.
I'd see her boys use their side door
to enter their kitchen with their girlfriends.
They'd always kid around with my son,
who was five-years-old, and they'd laugh
as he zoomed down the hill on his Big Wheel.

Sometimes, when my husband worked late,
I'd hear creaky noises in my house:
pipes groaning, water dripping
and imaginary noises in the cellar.
Then I'd open my drapes and see
Vivian and Jerry's kitchen light was still on.
They were probably playing Pinochle.
I'd feel as safe as when I was a little kid
knowing Mom and Dad were near by.
I kept my drapes open so their light
would shine down on my driveway.

This Love Affair With Dancing

began when I was only four
dancing on top
of my uncle's shoes
whirling round and round.
Then, in Ms. Barry's dance class
we tapped to "Crazy Rhythm,"
and rocked around the clock
at the school sock hop.
I longed to dance to the big band
sounds of Glen Miller
and Guy Lombardo,
but, I was born the wrong decade.
The 60s' ended
social partner dancing
beginning with The Twist.

Ballroom is back
with "Dancing with the Stars."
Every week I watch couples compete,
and thrill as they dance the Quickstep,
the Viennese Waltz, the torrid Tango.
My grandson notices my rapt attention.
He asks, "Would you like to dance

on that show?"

"Sure, if I were young."

I hold back tears, find joy in the music.

In my den, no one notices

I am dancing the Quickstep,

and as the music surges,

I leap like a deer.

Under Starry Skies

At camp we place our cots
on damp grass at night
outside our tents.
Crickets chirp in the cool air,
a breeze floats over us,
we're comfy under covers.
After gabbing and giggling,
we settle down and study
the black sky brimming
with sparkling stars brighter
than mom's diamond ring,
Aunt Matty's rhinestones.
Tonight, stars multiply
almost hiding the sky.
We look for the North Star
and The Big Dipper.
In the city, I've never seen
such a gem-filled sight.
Gail is crying in her tent,
still homesick.
I wish she would join us.
The stars would make her smile.
In my head, Roy Rogers sings

under starry skies above.
I try to stay awake
I want to gaze at the moon
'til I lose my senses
I don't want to sleep.
I want to stare, stare
at the starry sky,
stare at the starry sky.

Lost Gift

I want those days back
when I rowed alone
across the lake,
then pulled the oars out
to drift along
the inlets and coves.
I listened to waves
slip-slapping the boat,
while I wondered
about the boy back home.
What if he liked me?
What if he asked me out?
What if I said yes?

I want those days back.
The hours lost imagining
what could be
to behold what was:
the wonder of being
sixteen
filled with curiosity,
looking my best,
yet not knowing it.

I want to recapture
those days,
my eagerness to drift.

Wedding Day

I attempt to attend mass
on Thanksgiving morning,
but I am an hour too late.
It figures.
My father and brothers
are already in their tuxedos
excited about the big day.
My bridesmaids,
lovely in their hot pink gowns,
help me dress.
When we pose for pictures,
my father screams
at my brothers
for what I don't know.
It figures.
My brother hurries by
with tears in his eyes.
I am usually the first
to get upset and cry
about family scenes,
but I am as calm
as a country pond.
I know I'm leaving the sea

of family turmoil behind.
No one can make me
cry today.
I am about to marry
a kind, easy-going
young man,
and my spirit senses
freedom.
When the photographer
brings us our photos,
he comments,
 "I never saw a bride smile
as much as you did."
Who would've figured?

Why I Miss New Jersey

Because I feel at home back there
speaking with my Jersey accent.
And I know the roads: New Jersey
Turnpike, Garden State Parkway.

Because I miss my favorite neighbors
who became my good friends.
And my best friend still misses me
ever since we shared crushes on boys,
and shy first dances.

Because pizza tastes better
due to the water,
and all the Greek diners
have the best rice pudding.

Because I swam at Palisades Amusement
Park, roller skated at Columbia Rink,
and attended church dances.

Because I went dancing for the first time
with my husband at Molinari's night club,
before I knew he was the one.

Because Mom and Dad were together
back then, and my brothers' lives
held positive possibilities.

Because the beach at Wildwood is the widest
with the whitest sand, and Lake Hopatcong
with its forty-five miles of shoreline
is where I spent my teen summers working.

I'm comforted by the familiar landscape,
although some of the old neighborhood
looks like a ghetto now; I'm still connected.
Because I grew up and became
who I am there.

Young Heart

You see me at my desk
typing insurance claims.
My bifocals slide down
on my nose.
I'm dressed in my grey
polyester pantsuit.
You think,
"She's most likely
a grandma almost ready
to retire."
But you are unaware
that when I type
my mind travels:

I am the teenager pushed
off the dock into the lake
with all my clothes on
for the 100th time.
When I come up for air,
I still laugh with my friends.

I'm on the boardwalk
in Belmar with Mary.

We're both sunburned
and wearing identical
pedal pushers
searching for boys.

I'm at the Lore Lei
in New York City
dancing with a stranger
while the band plays,
"Moon River."

Now you're in on my secret.
I've discovered
the fountain of youth
even though
you see an older woman
typing insurance claims.

Message to a Condo Owner

Fort Lee, N.J.

On hot August nights,
when you sit on the balcony
of your condo
with your neighbors
longing for a breeze
to cool the humid air,
do you hear voices
of children and teenagers
vibrant and clear
as they whiz by
on The Flying Scooter
almost brushing
the trees' branches,
and shrieks from the riders
on the Cyclone?
Can you see the flirty couples
enter the doorway
of The Tunnel of Love?
Does your breath quicken
as the acrobat
balances himself
on the tightrope?

Are you enticed by the smell

of French fries sprinkled

with vinegar,

and saltwater

from the park's pool?

Can you hear the whir

of motor boats

as they circle

with colored flags flapping?

Does the carousel music

charm you?

Listen, feel, and enjoy

the happy spirits dwelling there.

Condo Owner, you are

on the holy grounds

of Palisades Amusement Park.

ABOUT THE AUTHOR

BARBARA EKNOIAN hails from New Jersey, and now resides in La Mirada, California with her extended family, but she's never forgotten her roots. She was the first recipient of the Jane Buel Bradley Chapbook Award in 2002 and was published by Pearl Editions. Her young adult novel, *Chances Are: A Jersey Girl Comes of Age* has been recently released at Amazon.

If you enjoyed this book you might also enjoy:

CHANCES ARE: A JERSEY GIRL COMES OF AGE

BARBARA EKNOIAN

It's the l950s'. Teenager, Susie Di Pietro, lives near the projects in New Jersey. Bookies stand on the corner by the candy store and sound like characters from Guys and Dolls. Everyone plays the numbers, even young Susie.

Throughout her high school years, she's painfully aware that her pal, Ginger, and she are wallflowers. Susie shares her romantic tribulations, her trials with her teachers, and funny incidents that happen to her while she is growing up.

Chances Are is a charming coming-of-age novel that will take you on a nostalgic trip: dancing to Johnny Mathis, Elvis, and The Platters. It will trigger fond memories for some readers of their teen years, and give younger readers a picture of that special era, "The Fifties."

Available at Amazon, Kindle, and select bookstores